Orphan

The Story of a Baby Woodchuck

Orphan

The Story of a Baby Woodchuck

by Faith McNulty

illustrated by Darby Morrell

SCHOLASTIC INC.
NEW YORK

Library of Congress Cataloging-in-Publication Data

McNulty, Faith.
    Orphan: the story of a baby woodchuck / by Faith McNulty;
illustrated by Darby Morrell.
        p. cm.
    Summary: The author describes finding an orphaned baby woodchuck
and caring for it until it was able to fend for itself in the wild again.
    ISBN 0-590-43838-7
    1. Marmots — Anecdotes — Juvenile literature. [1. Woodchuck.
2. Wildlife rescue.] I. Morrell, Darby, ill. II. Title.
QL795.M3M36   1992
599.32′32 — dc20   91-25333
                                                                         CIP
                                                                          AC

12 11 10 9 8 7 6 5 4 3 2 1   2 3 4 5 6 7/9

Printed in the U.S.A.   37

First Scholastic printing, May 1992

Book design by Laurie McBarnette

I live in Rhode Island in a farmhouse surrounded by meadows and woods. I share the farm with lots of animals: deer, rabbits, coyotes, foxes, raccoons, possums, skunks, and woodchucks, to name just a few. I am aware that hundreds of animal lives are being lived close to me, and yet, most of the time, we do not meet. Each kind of animal, me included, lives in its own private world. Now and then our paths cross. In winter, on a snowy morning, I see mouse tunnels under the snow and rabbit tracks

everywhere. In the spring I hear frogs peeping in the pond, and find the footprints of raccoons, possums, and foxes in the soft mud. Sometimes deer graze in the meadow beyond my kitchen window.

Before the grass grows too high, I often see a woodchuck on a little hill in the meadow. It is a small, brown animal, about the size of a big, fat cat, but rounder and plumper, with very short legs.

Woodchucks are related to squirrels, but are much larger. They are plant eaters who divide their time between the meadows, where they feed, and a deep burrow that they dig in the earth, in which they sleep and raise their young.

From time to time the woodchuck I see from my window sits up on its haunches, the better to look around for danger. Dogs, foxes, and coyotes love to eat woodchucks. They can easily kill a chuck if they catch it away from its burrow. Woodchucks understand the danger of predators and are wary, but they do not understand man-made dangers. While crossing highways to go from one feeding spot to another, they sometimes run in front of cars and are killed.

One spring day I walked out my driveway to the mailbox on the highway and noted the body of a woodchuck by the roadside. *Too bad*, I thought. I started home and stopped short. A little woodchuck, all alone, was hurrying along the driveway. Nose raised, he looked as though he had an urgent appointment just ahead. I had a strong feeling he was looking for his mother, and that it was her body that lay in the weeds.

The little brown fellow, who was not much bigger than my shoe, hustled bravely along on his short legs, unaware that a towering giant was watching him and wondering what to do. It isn't always the best thing to pick up a wild orphan. If there is any chance a little animal can rejoin its mother, it is best to leave it alone; but in this case, I felt the orphan had no chance of making it on his own. I guessed that when the mother did not return to the nest, hunger had driven the babies out into the world much too soon.

I was wearing a sweater over my blouse. I took it off, threw it over the chuck, and picked him up wrapped in its folds. I feared he might try to bite, but he only gave a little snort and burrowed into my arms. I walked on, holding him care-

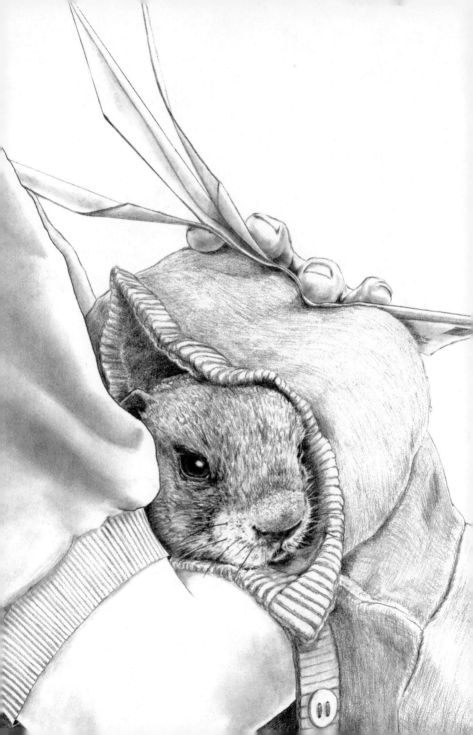

fully. Though I was a grown woman, I was excited in a way I hadn't been since I was a child, when animals, especially wild pets, were what I thought about most and always wanted more of.

At home I put the chuck in the bathtub to keep him from getting lost in the house while I took time to think. He scrabbled at the slippery porcelain, trying to climb out. I knew he must be very scared and probably very hungry, too. I threw a towel over him. He hid his head in its folds and was quiet. I stroked his coarse fur. *Poor little woodchuck*, I thought. *You are so small in a world that is so much bigger than you will ever know!* And then I thought, *Oh, my gosh, what am I going to do with him now?*

When I was a child, my mother helped me care for several orphan babies — robins, mice, and rabbits — and the bathroom had been a convenient nursery. Chuck could stay here, I decided, but he needed a more comfortable bed.

I found a cardboard carton and put cat litter in the bottom and a layer of hay on top of it. I lifted Chuck in. He dived gratefully into the hay. Now I needed to figure out how to feed him. What could I substitute for woodchuck milk?

There are books about the care of wild orphans, and I happened to have one on my shelves. Most baby mammals, it said, can be fed a mixture of baby cereal, dry skim milk, and water dripped from a medicine dropper. I prepared Chuck's first meal and took it to the bathroom.

I picked Chuck up and put him in my lap. He struggled in my grasp. I held him tight, gently pressed the medicine dropper into his mouth, and squeezed. As he tasted the food Chuck froze, as though stunned with surprise. He swallowed hesitantly, then sucked frantically at the end of the dropper. The dropperful went down fast. Then too fast! Chuck choked, and milk

bubbled out of his nose. I thought, *Oh, gosh! I've drowned him!* but he sneezed, wiped his nose with his paws, and nuzzled about searching for the magic fountain of food. Soon I learned to squeeze at the rate he could swallow. And so our life as adopted mother and child began.

Chuck trusted me quickly. When I put my hands into the box to lift him, he rushed to them eagerly, making a strange little chuckling noise. He drank greedily. Two ounces filled him. Then he slept, sometimes curled up in the hay, sometimes on his back with his legs flung out, showing his round, babyish belly. Awake, he often played, rolling around and biting at the hay. He liked to nibble my fingers and wrestle with them, kicking against my hand the way kittens do.

Holding him, I observed him closely. At first, when I picked him up, I had thought he was homely as a burlap bag. I had pitied him for

being a mere woodchuck. He would never be
graceful or very bright; never be swift or beautiful. He would always be a chunky, brown fellow
with coarse fur, short legs, and a taste for the
depths of the earth.

As I held him five or six times a day, he
became beautiful.

I noticed his hands. They were black, with
four long fingers ending in strong, curved nails
and a tiny thumb. His hands were made for

Peering out of tunnel

Front track

Whiskers for gauging
width of tunnels.

Teeth continue to grow
throughout the Woodchuck's
life. Keeps the teeth the right
length by constantly chewing.

Thumb, 3/8 of an inch long

Nail on third
digit, left hand

digging, but he also used them cleverly, like a squirrel, to pick up and hold things. Sometimes he wrapped four fingers around one of mine the way human babies do.

The color of his fur was a mixture of gray and tan beneath long, bristly guard hairs banded in black and white, giving a tweedy effect. His shoulders, upper arms, and lower flanks were foxy red. His belly was dark, the color of coffee beans.

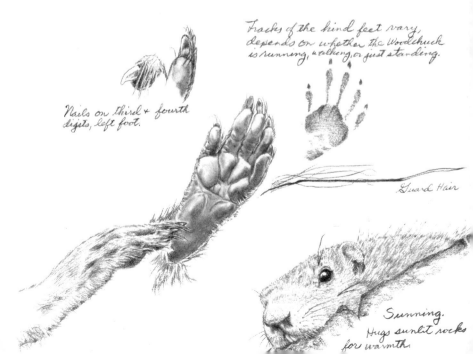

Nails on third + fourth digits, left foot.

Tracks of the hind feet vary, depends on whether the Woodchuck is running, walking, or just standing.

Guard Hair

Sunning.
Hugs sunlit rocks for warmth.

I noted his ears: small, round squirrel ears, neat and appropriate to a life spent partly in tunnels. His eyes were oval and set near the top of his skull to give good upward vision. They were dark as raisins and softly shiny. There were whiskers by his nose, and another set on his cheeks. They would be useful to check the diameter of tunnels. His body ended in a rather meager tail, neither long nor short; but nevertheless I thought it was a very nice tail.

Packed into this small body was amazing energy and will. As he struggled to get every drop of milk, I felt he was saying, "I am a woodchuck and I want to live." Then I realized that by trusting me, by chuckling at me, and nibbling me, he was also saying, "I am *your* woodchuck. My life is in your hands."

Soon the original carton seemed too small. I let him free to roam the bathroom. As a retreat I gave him a box with a round doorway cut in the

front. He knew instantly that a hole spells home and dashed inside. I put cat litter in a pan nearby. Chuck instinctively understood its purpose. He used it without any teaching by me.

Now that he was free he became wary. Any sudden noise sent him flying into his house. At first the sight of me scared him, too, but his fear soon wore off and he would greet me eagerly, scrabbling at my ankles and trying to climb up my legs.

His scratching hurt, so I would pick him up and cradle him. Then he would nibble my hand with gentle bites, chuckling with excitement and affection. His long, curved front teeth could have hurt me, but he was always careful. When I put him down he usually squeaked in protest, and if I left the bathroom door open he followed, making an urgent little noise that sounded like, "Don't leave me! Don't leave me! I want to come, too!"

*   *   *

I decided I would like to know more about the life of wild woodchucks, so I looked them up at my library. There are woodchucks almost everywhere in the United States, I found, except in the Deep South. In the West they are called marmots.

The life of a woodchuck revolves around its burrow. This is much more than a hole in the ground. It is a tunnel, up to thirty feet long, with several chambers. The dirt of the excavation is heaped into a mound from which the woodchuck can view the landscape. There is also a back door, dug from underneath and hardly visible. If the front door is under siege, the chuck can escape out the back. If threatened above ground, it can plunge down the back door; thus the back door increases the area in which a woodchuck can feed without being too far from safety.

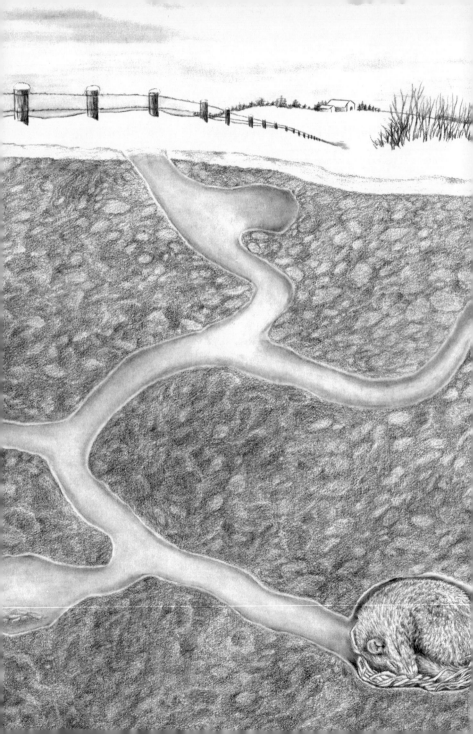

Just inside the burrow there is a wide place for turning around. Deeper down is a nest chamber lined with soft grass, and near it is a toilet chamber used only for this purpose.

Woodchucks are famous for their ability to sleep through the winter. When autumn comes and their food supply begins to wither, each chuck digs a new den in a safe place. There it curls up and sinks into a sleep so deep it doesn't awaken even if disturbed. In one experiment, a tame woodchuck that was dug out and handled while asleep did not open its eyes. In this state, called hibernation, the chuck uses very little energy and needs no food. It breathes very slowly, once every six minutes, and its heartbeat is equally slow. Its body becomes cold, about fifty degrees Fahrenheit, but not frozen.

When the chuck wakes up it has lost about a third of its body weight, but it is strong and healthy, ready to begin a new season of eating and storing fat.

When the cycle of woodchuck life begins in the spring, the males wander about, looking for females. The females stay at home, waiting to be courted. Tail wagging, a male checks each den he comes across. If a female accepts him, he moves in with her and they mate. She lets him stay awhile, but not long. The young will be born thirty days after the mating. As the birthday nears, the female drives the male away. He is allowed no part in raising their children.

There are usually four babies. They are born tiny, blind, and hairless, but they grow rapidly. At six weeks they are fat, furry, and playful. One day the mother leads them up the tunnel and they discover the vast, green world above-ground. They sun themselves and play at the entrance, but do not go far.

This is the only social time in the life of a woodchuck. As adults they will always live apart. Their babyhood ends when they are so big that the nest is crowded. Then the mother separates them, leading each to a new den dug nearby. Now the young chucks must learn to live alone. The separation is gradual. The mother visits each young one often, suckling and grooming and comforting it.

At this point the young chuck is also learning about the two most important things in woodchuck life: food and danger. Mother and young one feed together. She chooses the tastiest, most nutritious plants among the meadow grasses. The youngster follows her example. If the mother shows alarm, the young one follows her in a dive for safety and thus learns to fear predators.

As the young woodchucks become prepared to face life alone, the mother's visits taper off. One day she doesn't come at all. No one knows what the young chucks think or feel, but we do know that after a few days alone they move off,

perhaps to look for their mother, perhaps to explore the world. Soon each one digs a burrow and its adult life begins. Its main occupation is eating and storing fat. Among the dangers it faces are angry farmers. Woodchucks love fruit and vegetables and know nothing of private property. A woodchuck can make short work of a row of vegetables, to the chagrin of the legal owner. Sometimes farmers shoot woodchucks or throw poison gas bombs down their burrows.

When a woodchuck has stored enough fat, it seeks a sheltered place where leaves carpet the ground and the frost does not go deep. There it digs a new den and goes to sleep.

Having learned how woodchucks live in the wild, I had a clearer idea of what I must do to be a good mother. First of all I needed to start teaching Chuck to eat wild plants. That wasn't easy. I offered Chuck all sorts of grasses, fruit, and vegetables. He would taste them, look disgusted, and chuckle urgently for milk. I finally persuaded him to eat a cherry and a marigold, but that was it.

I realized, too, that he needed to learn more about the world he would live in: about plants, damp earth, and dangerous dogs. I took him outside and put him on the lawn. At the sight of the open sky, he showed sheer terror, flattening himself against the ground. I brought his box outside. He dashed into it and refused to come out. Obviously the experiment had failed. I brought Chuck back to the bathroom.

I went on offering tempting meals of flowers and grasses. He let them wilt untouched, and climbed into my lap as eagerly as ever for a feeding of milk. He was getting bigger every day. I had a very spoiled woodchuck on my hands.

At last I decided to do what mother woodchucks do: put him in a new burrow and leave him. I searched along the wall of our orchard and found a hole in the earth. I decided to take a chance no other animal was living in it. I put Chuck in his box near the hole. I laid a bouquet of clover and young carrots nearby and left. I knew that eventually hunger would force Chuck to leave the box and perhaps to taste the food, too.

I worried through the next few hours. He was still my baby. I didn't want to part with him until I felt sure he could make it. I fixed a meal of milk and cereal and went to the orchard. His box was empty. I called, "Chuck!" and within seconds Chuck dashed out of the hole and flung himself on my ankles, chuckling gladly. Glad, too, I sat down and fed him and let him snuggle in my arms.

Getting away wasn't easy. He raced after me, and since I didn't want him sitting on my doorstep I had to lead him back. Eventually I escaped by putting him on the far side of the wall so that he couldn't see me walk away.

The next day I visited and fed him several times. He greeted me joyfully and drank gratefully. A few days later he began to nibble carrots and daisies. I was thrilled that he was being weaned at last. In a few more days he refused

milk, though he greeted me as eagerly as ever. Sometimes he was quite far from the hole, but he came galloping at the sound of my voice. As I sat on the grass he would climb into my lap and we would groom each other: he nibbling me gently, me stroking him with my fingers. It felt strange to have a lonely little woodchuck cling to me so desperately. I wondered if wild chucks tried as hard to keep their mothers' waning interest.

We parted unexpectedly. I went away on a brief trip. When I came back, I went to the orchard and called. No woodchuck came. I felt a sudden loss. I had wanted to say good-bye. I comforted myself with the thought that he didn't need me anymore. I imagined him journeying out to the green and fragrant fields, eating clover and alfalfa, and leading a happy woodchuck life.

The story should end there, but it doesn't. Nothing I read in books about woodchucks suggested that they ever return to their first home, so I supposed I would never see Chuck again. The summer wore on. The woodchucks I glimpsed from the kitchen window were sleek and fat; sitting on their haunches they looked like little bears. I wondered if one of them was mine, but there was no way to tell. Watching them, I remembered fondly the good feeling of having been close to this funny little furry person; and of caring for him, and having him love me back.

Now golden October days were followed by chill, dark nights. Leaves littered the little garden beside my front door. I was working there one day when I raised my eyes to see a huge woodchuck ambling confidently up the flagstone path. He headed straight for me, chuckling a greeting, and then he tried to scramble up my leg, just like old times.

I bent to pick him up, but the sight of his huge front teeth stopped me. If he became frightened he could inflict a terrible bite. I gently detached myself and went inside to think. I realized that I couldn't let him stay. It wouldn't be safe for him or for me. If he remained tame and trusting he might be killed by a dog or a car. I couldn't take him into the house for his winter sleep. Even my cellar would be too warm. Though I hated to turn him away, I knew that Chuck would have to go back to the wild.

I had a large trap in my cellar. Called a Havahart, it is a box made of wire mesh with a front end that closes when an animal goes inside. It catches an animal without hurting it. I put a carrot in the trap and took it outside. Chuck was waiting. I put the trap down and sat beside it. Chuck ambled over to me. He sniffed and nibbled my hand. I touched him ever so gently and said, "This time it really *is* good-bye."

Chuck spied the carrot in the trap and walked in. The door snapped shut. Chuck looked startled and confused. I picked up the trap. It was heavy; he must have weighed ten or twelve pounds. As I lifted the trap, Chuck gave a scream and crouched in terror. I felt the way any mother would who has betrayed her child.

I put the trap in my car and drove along a

farm road to a hay field half a mile from the house. It was a good woodchuck place, lots to eat and far from cars. I stopped at the edge of the field and put the cage on the ground. I opened the door and Chuck rushed out, racing toward the tall grass.

He didn't look back. He was a wild wood-chuck at last.